GARY JONES

Boston

Contents

Introduction

I want to thank you and congratulate you for downloading the book, "Boston Travel Guide: How to Make The Most Out of Your 3-Day Boston Vacation".

Boston is a paradise for intellectuals. It is the home of various revolutionary sites, as well as the beloved John F. Kennedy. The city is also well-known as the Athens of America. It boasts of towering urban monoliths, prestigious universities, and captivating architectural gems. It's a city of dreams and opportunities. Boston is a city with an alluring past, electrifying present, and a dazzling future. It's a city that you should definitely visit at least once in your lifetime.

Boston is an East Coast paradise. It's surrounded by the sea, but this quaint and beautiful city is the center of the political, cultural, and social life. The city played a huge role in the American Revolution and you will find many memorials, and traces of this event in history throughout it.

The city offers intriguing narrow streets that tell stories about the revolution and the country's transformation. It is a city of poets, philosophers, preachers, scientists, and scholars. It may be filled with history, but it is also the home of modern architectural treasures. You will find fascinating bookstores, intimidating universities, historical buildings, stunning parks, enchanting museums, and the famous swan boats.

This book is your ultimate Greater Boston travel guide. It contains valuable information that you can use to make your Boston trip more enjoyable—making sure that you don't miss a thing. This book also comes with a list of the best restaurants, hotels, museums, and landmarks that you should include in your travel itinerary.

In this book, you'll learn:

- Boston's rich history and the role it plays in the American revolution
- When's the best time to visit this scenic metropolitan area
- How to get around the area
- The best budget-friendly hotels
- The best restaurants and foods to try
- The most amazing and visually stimulating museums
- The best coffee shops
- The vibrant Boston nightlife
- Unique things that you can only do in Boston
- Tips that you can use in organizing a day trip to Cambridge (the home of the most prestigious universities in the world and one of the most popular areas in Great Boston area)
- Safety and travel tips
- Insider tips
- And more!

We also provide you with a pre-planned three day itinerary that you can use to get the most out of your Boston vacation. You will find tips that can help you explore the city of Boston like a local.

Boston is an energetic city. It's no New York, but it's also a city where dreams come true. It is a place where many ambitious students choose to get a college education. It is a friendly and warm cultural melting pot that welcomes people from different cultures and races with open arms. It is an inventive city that's filled with interesting views, thought-provoking artwork, and great restaurants that offer a unique gastronomical experience.

It's one of the most progressive cities in the world and yet, it has a warm small-town vibe. It is a beautiful city with massive cultural value and historical significance. It's a city that you should see at least once in your lifetime.

Thank you again for downloading this book and I hope that you enjoy it!

1

Boston in a Nutshell

Boston is the center of a metropolitan area called the Greater Boston. It is the capital of Massachusetts and the most progressive city in the New England region. It is also one of the oldest cities in the United States. The city is best known as the cradle of liberty as it's the birthplace of the American Revolution.

This beautiful city lies on the Massachusetts Bay. You would be able to see the Atlantic Ocean from the east side of the city. Known as the paradise for intellectuals and academics, a huge percentage of its residents are actually students. It is a city filled with scientific innovation and engaging discourse.

Boston has a vibrant and electrifying atmosphere, an impressive skyline, and is very easy to navigate. It is also often called the "walking city" because you can go around the city by foot. The best bit is that there's plenty of things to see and do while you walk. For sports fans, they recognize the city as the home of the two of the most popular sports teams in the United States – the Red Sox and the Celtics.

Here are a few of interesting facts about Boston:

- It is the home of the oldest park in the United States – the Boston Common. This stunning park was established in 1634 and used to be an execution site.

- It has a tunnel that's 90 feet below the ground. The Ted Williams Tunnel was opened in 1995 and was named after Red Sox player Ted Williams.
- The early settlers in the city came from Boston, England. That's how it got its name.
- The city has two mega skyscrapers – the John Hancock Tower and the Prudential Tower.
- It's the home of the Little Brewster Island – the site where the first ever lighthouse in the United States was built.
- Boston's Tremont Street Subway is the first subway system in the United States.
- Boston is indeed the city of many firsts. It is also the home of Revere Beach, the first public beach in the United States.
- This "City on the Hill" is the hometown of many Hollywood superstars, including James Spader, Mark Wahlberg, Matt Damon, and Barbara Walters.
- The Boston Public Library was established in 1849, making it the oldest public library in the country.
- Boston is also home to some of the most powerful men in the United States, including George W. Bush, Benjamin Franklin, and John F. Kennedy.

JFK Statue Boston

- This city is not a big fan of fast food. It has more than eight hundred restaurants and yet, only forty out of that number serves fastfood.
- Boston has over a hundred universities and colleges. This is the reason why it's called the "Athens of America".
- The city also has the first ever fire department in the United States.
- The first ever Thanksgiving was celebrated in Boston in 1621.
- Boston is the home of the oldest functioning commissioned ship in the United States – the U.S.S. Constitution. It now serves as a museum.
- Boston is the site for the first witch execution, before the Salem Witch Trials.

Boston is indeed one of the most beautiful and interesting cities in the United States. Its streets are lined with cherry blossoms during spring time, but it looks like a white wonderland during winter. It is eclectic yet progressive, and is home to some of the most brilliant minds in the United States.

Boston's Rich History

Boston is sometimes called the "Cradle of Liberty" because of it played a huge role in the birth of the American Revolution.

Boston used to be home to the Massachusetts Native Americans. It was once called "Shawmut" which means "living water". Shawmut was blessed with three hills, namely Beacon Hill, Mount Vernon, and Pemberton Hill.

Captain John Smith sailed to the Massachusetts Bay in 1614 and befriended the Native Americans living in that area. He later published a map, renaming the place: "New England".

In 1623, the settlement in the Georges colony failed. All of the colonists went back to Britain, except for one – William Blackstone. He moved to Shawmut, making him the first white resident of Boston. The location where Blackstone was known to have built his cabin can be located in the intersection of the Beacon Street and Charles Street.

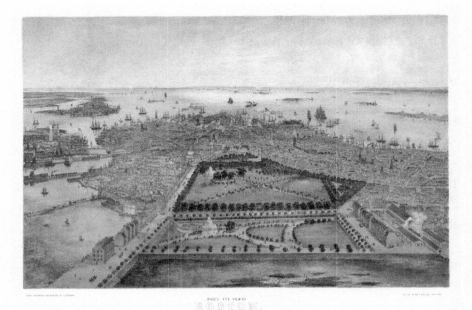

Boston 1850

In 1930, the Puritans arrived. This set of colonists were trying to avoid religious persecution in Britain and was led by an English lawyer named John Winthrop. Most of these Puritans came from Boston, Lincolnshire in England. And so, they renamed the area "Boston".

After a few years, the Massachusetts Bay colony began to expand and soon, the colonists built the first ever public school in America – the Boston Latin School.

In 1634, slaves from Africa arrived in Boston. This began an era of the slavery in Massachusetts.

In 1675, King Phillip launched a war to wipe out the Native American tribes.

The ones who survived the war fled or were sold as slaves. This was a violent and tragic period in Boston's history—many of the natives died during it and some were even completely wiped out by the colonists who sought to drive them out of their own land.

Despite the genocide of the natives, Boston continued to grow over the years. By 1975, what was once a small colony on a hill has become the home to fifteen thousand people.

By 1765, Britain was experiencing an economic problem. And so, the British government decided to collect huge taxes from the colonists to help pay off the country's debt. This angered the colonists, of course. In response, a group called "Sons of Liberty" began to stage protests. This increased the tension between the British forces and the colonists.

On March 5, 1770, a young wigmaker named Edward Garrick confronted Captain Lieutenant John Goldfinch over an unpaid bill. But, Goldfinch had already paid the bill, so he simply ignored the wigmaker's demands. A young soldier, a man we know as Private White, pointed out Garrick's disrespectful behavior promptly. This, of course, led to a fight—with White eventually hitting Garrick with his musket.

This act of violence angered the Bostonians.

Within a few hours, a mob of angry colonists attacked the British soldiers, throwing stones and cursing at them. The British officers eventually fired their rifles in response, killing five colonists.

This was a turning point in American history. After the incident, more and more colonists pushed for independence. The members of Sons of Liberty began to secretly organize meetings and planned protests against the oppressive British government.

When the British government decided to impose heavy taxes on tea, the colonists threw out three hundred forty two chests of British tea into the sea as a sign of protest. This event was called the Boston Tea Party and was considered as their first major act of defiance against the British Government.

On April 1775, Paul Revere rode a horse in the middle of the night to warn the colonists that the British army has arrived in America. This was the beginning of the American Revolution.

Today, Boston continues to be the most progressive city in the United States. It's a symbol of strength, resilience, and patriotism. It's truly the "cradle of liberty".

2

When's The Best Time to Visit?

Boston has a little of everything. It's perfect for history buffs as it has over three hundred historic sites within the city. It also has more than fifty historical landmarks that you can visit. Aside from this, they also have dozens of beautiful museums and a must-visit arcade called Black Bay. But, while they have all of these things to offer, you wouldn't be able to enjoy them if the weather is a little unfriendly for roaming around.

So, what's the weather in Boston like?

Boston Weather and Seasonal Activities

Boston has a generally humid climate. Like most cities in the United States, Boston has four seasons – winter, spring, summer, and autumn.

- **Summer**

Summer in Boston starts around June and ends in August. During summertime, Boston is warm, though the first weeks of June can be rainy, cold, and chilly. But, in July and August, the temperature can range from 15 degree Celsius and 26 degree Celsius. Most days are hot, but some days are a bit rainy, so make sure that you pack a compact umbrella that you can carry around during the day.

If you're visiting Boston during the summertime, be sure to ride the Boston Swan Boats. This is also a great season to walk the Freedom Trail.

Aside from the above, there are a number of other seasonal activities during summer:

- North End Feasts
- Boston Harborfest
- Independence Day Celebration
- Taste of Cambridge
- Summer Concerts

You can also enjoy a bit of whale watching on the Stellwagen Bank which is just twenty five miles away from downtown Boston. You can also do the "Boston Hop on Hop off" tours. It's also the best time to see a Red Sox game at the Fenway Park or if you want something more relaxed, a brunch cruise would be just as great.

11

· Spring

Spring starts around March and ends in May. March can still be a bit rainy, so be sure to pack your sweater, boots, and umbrella. The flowers begin to bloom come April. But, you would still be able to see blossoming cherry trees and magnolias around the city by May. The streets of downtown Boston are a sight to see during the springtime. There are also a number of fun activities during springtime in Boston, you can choose from:

- · ArtWeek
- · Boston Calling (An eclectic music festival)
- · Boston Pride
- · Dragon Boat Festival
- · Cambridge Art River Festival
- · Boston Red Sox Opening Day
- · Patriot's Day
- · Boston Marathon

- LGBT Film Festival
- Cambridge Science Festival

Fall

Boston, aside from its many cultural offerings, also has a fascinating landscape. It also has a number of architectural wonders. Among the many different seasons, many would agree that autumn is most beautiful in this city.

It is a time when the whole city is filled with vibrant colors. The trees and streets are covered with red, yellow, brown, and orange trees. It's dazzling and absolutely stunning.

Autumn starts in September and ends in October. The whole city's temperature remains cool during fall season, so don't forget to pack jackets, boots, and umbrellas. It's also quite gloomy during the day and it can get cold at night.

There are a lot of autumn activities in Boston, including:

- Boston Arts Festival
- Boston Local Food Festival
- Berklee Beantown Jazz Festival
- Boston Book Festival

- **Winter**

Winter starts around December and ends in March. Boston can get really cold during the winter time. The city sometimes experiences freezing cold winds and even snow storms.

The winter weather in Boston is a bit unpredictable. Some winter days are sunny. But, some days are just crazy cold. When you're traveling to Boston during the winter season, don't forget to pack warm socks, gloves, scarf, hat, coat, and waterproof boots.

There are a lot of events in Boston during the winter time, including:

- Boston Wine Festival
- Chinese New Year
- First Night First Day
- Black History Month

If you are from a tropical state or country, you might want to think twice about visiting Boston during winter time as you may have a hard time coping with the extreme cold temperatures.

Boston Weather by Month

Boston is generally a chilly city. But, it also tends to vary quite a bit. To give you a better idea on what to wear and what to bring when you visit, below is a list of the average Boston temperatures per month:

Month Average Temperature in Celsius

January -2 degrees

February -1 degrees

March 3 degrees

April 11 degrees

May 17 degrees

June 22 degrees

July 24 degrees

August 25 degrees

September 18 degrees

October 14 degrees

November 8 degrees

December 3 degrees

What is The Best Month to Visit Boston?

The best time to visit Boston is between June to October. It is fun to do various walking tours around summer time. It's also a good time to take a cruise and walk around the city. If you want to see Boston in all its sunny glory, visit between June and August. But, the city can get crowded and hotel rates also skyrocket high during summertime. So, if you want to avoid the crowds and get good hotel rates, visit the city on September or October. As mentioned earlier, Boston is absolutely stunning during the fall season. The colors and landscapes are absolutely sensational.

If you decide to visit Boston from June to October, don't forget to catch the following events – Boston Pride Parade (June), Cambridge Arts River Festival (June), Boston Fireworks Spectacular (July), Boston Harbor Fest (July), Boston Film Festival (September), Boston Comic Con (August), and Oktoberfest (October).

3

How to Get Around Boston

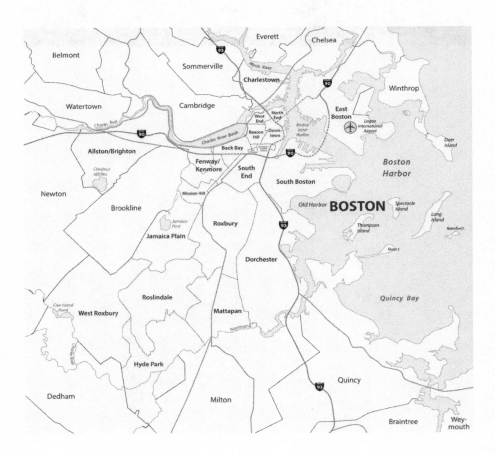

If you are arriving in Boston By Plane then you will be landing at the Logan International Airport.

Boston is a "walkable" city, so one of the best ways to see it is by foot. Being quite a compact city, you could easily walk to almost anywhere you want to go. But if you're unable to, the city also has an advanced and efficient transportation system that will provide you with utmost convenience during your visit.

The public transport system (buses, trains) is operated by the Massachusetts Bay Transportation Authority or MBTA. The trains under MBTA are called "T". If you plan to take the train or the bus, you should get a Charlie Card, the payment method for MBTA buses and trains. It's a reloadable plastic card that you can use to pay for bus and train fares. The best bit is that you can use your debit or credit card to reload this card should you run out of credits.

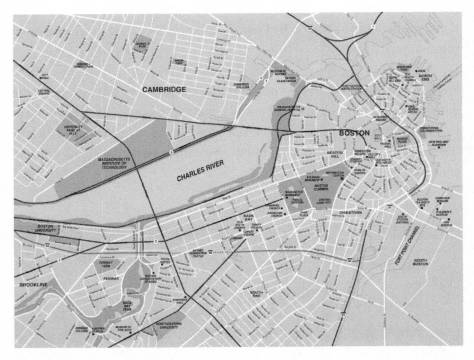

Why you should get a Charlie Card? Well, Charlie Card holders pay lower fares and it saves you a lot of time—enabling you to avoid long queues. You can easily get a blank card for free from an MBTA agent at train and bus stations around Boston.

The Boston Subway is made up of four lines – the Blue Line, the Orange Line, the Red Line, and the Green Line.

- The Red Line is will take you to Harvard University.
- The Orange Line runs along the Orange Street, now known as Washington Street.
- The Blue Line runs along the Boston Harbor.
- The Green Line runs along the some part of the Emerald Necklace (Boston Common, Public Garden, The Fens, the Commonwealth Avenue Mall,

Franklin Park, and Jamaica Pond) and into the suburban areas of Newton and Brookline.

The basic fare for one train ride is $2.75 if you're using a Charlie ticket. But, it costs only $2.25 if you're using a Charlie Card.

If you're in a hurry, you could also opt to take the cab. You can easily hail a cab from Fenway Park and around the Boston Common area. However, it's best to call in advance and ask for a pick-up.

There are seven major cab companies in Boston:

- City Cab - phone(617) 536-5100.
- Top Cab - phone (617) 266-4800.
- ITOA Cab - phone (617)-268-1313.
- Metro Cab -phone (617)-782-5500.
- 617 Taxi Cab - phone (617)-829-4222.
- Tunnel Cab -phone (617) 567-2700.
- Boston Cab -phone 617-536-5010.

There are also pedicabs (pedal powered rickshaws) in the area if you want a more touristy type of transportation.

The bus is another great option for transportation. The city buses are operated by MBTA. There are more than 700 hundred bus routes in the city. From the airport, you can take the SL1 (Silver Line Bus) from Logan Airport to the South Station Bus Terminal.

Out of the seven hundred bus routes, here's a list of the most popular MBTA bus routes:

- Route #1 – Harvard to Dudley Station via the Massachusetts Avenue
- Route #22 – Ashmont Station to Ruggles Station via Jackson Square and Talbot Avenue
- Route #23 – Ashmont Station to Ruggles Station through Washington Street.
- Route #15 – Kane Square to Ruggle Station via Savin Hill, Hancock Street, Uphams Corner, Malcolm X Boulevard, Roxbury Crossing, and Tremont Street.
- Route #39 – Forest Hills to Back Bar through Huntington Avenue.

If you're heading to Fenway Park take the routes CT3, CT1, CT2, 1, 19, 8, 55, 47, 65, and 60. But, if you're traveling to New York and other cities, head to the South Station located at 700 Atlantic Avenue. You can check the bus schedules at MBTA.com.

You can also rent a bike. The city has a hubway system (now officially known as Blue Bikes) that allows locals and tourists to grab a bike at one station and then return it at their destination.

4

Best Budget-Friendly Hotels in Boston

For the most part, most people tend to assume that Boston is an expensive city to visit. This might be true in certain cases, especially if you visit during peak seasons where even the cheapest hotels can cost a lot more than the hotels in Berlin, Athens, or even the hostels in New York City. But, don't let that discourage you from visiting. Boston does have plenty to offer in terms of affordable accommodations, you just have to know where to look!

HI Boston Hostel
 Address: 19 Stuart St, Boston
 Phone :+1 617-536-9455

The HI Boston Hostel is located at 19 Stuart Street, Theatre District. It is just as a few steps away from the historical buildings and from the Boston Common. It's also a short walk away from the Fenway Park.

If you're on a budget, this is a great option for you to look into. A bed costs $49.50 per night. It is perfect for solo travelers as the atmosphere is very social. They also provide a shared kitchen, too, where you can cook and eat.

This three star hotel is cozy and is a great place to make new friends. It's got a café, a bike storage area, a small library, and even a billiard table. This hotel will give you good value for your money.

Boston Omni Parker House Hotel
 Address: 60 School St, Boston
 Phone:+1 617-227-8600

The Boston Omni Parker House is considered as the oldest continuously operating hotel in America. This building was built by Harvey Parker in 1855. It has been the home of many famous guests as well as employees. The Vietnamese revolutionary leader Ho Chi Minh worked as a baker in this hotel from 1912 to 1913. Human rights activist Malcolm X also worked there as a busboy in the 1940s. Emeril Lagasse worked as a cook in the hotel kitchen before he became a superstar chef.

This hotel has a star-studded list of former guests, including Babe Ruth,

Franklin Delano Roosevelt, Bill Clinton, Colin Powell, Rachael Ray, Ben Affleck, James Dean, and Judy Garland. This hotel also served as the meeting place for some of America's literary geniuses, including Ralph Waldo Emerson, Charles Francis Adams, and Nathaniel Hawthorne.

The rooms can be quite expensive and can cost at least $389. But, you could get a room for as low as $240 if you book through Booking.com.

Hotel 140

Address: 140 Clarendon St, Boston

Phone: +1 617-585-5600

Hotel 140 is located at 140 Clarendon Street in Back Bay, Boston. It has a classic exterior made of bricks. Its façade has three arches and balconies that exude elegance and sophistication.

This hotel has a clean and well-polished exterior. The halls are simple and neat. The simplicity of this hotel is just captivating. The rooms are comfortable and cozy. Rooms cost at least $224 a night.

Kimpton Onyx Hotel

Address: 155 Portland St, Boston

Phone: +1 617-557-9955

This luxury four star hotel is located at 155 Portland Street, West End. It's only two minutes away from the Boston North Station. It has a modern and grand façade. It has a classy and yet, elegant interior. It has a luxurious bar and restaurant where you could eat good food, drink a delicious cocktail, or just stare at the lovely chandeliers hanging from the ceiling. This gym also has a fitness center.

The Kimpton Onyx Hotel is pet friendly, too, and it's great for the entire family. The rooms are comfortable, clean, and a great place to rest after doing lengthy tourist tours around Boston. Rooms cost at least $231 if you book via Booking.com

Wyndham Boston

Address: 5 Blossom St, Boston

Phone: +1 617-742-7630

This grand four star hotel is located in the posh neighborhood of Beacon Hill. It's one of the most prominent hotels in the city. It has a modern interior that looks slick, clean, and elegant. The rooms are filled with earth colors that instantly make you feel at home. It has a polished bar and high-class restaurant where you could dine and also hang out. It also has function rooms that are perfect for special events and even weddings. It also has an immaculate fitness center where you could exercise before doing tourist tours.

The rooms cost at least $237, but it's worth every penny.

5

Culinary Arcadias in Boston

Boston is home to some beloved American classics such as bacon burgers, cheesy pizzas, cream pies, lobster rolls, roast beef sandwiches, steaks, oysters, fried clams, ribeye, and roasted lamb. It is quite a culinary paradise.

Boston also has a wide array of restaurants that would fit every budget. So, whether you're up for something cheap yet cheerful or something more indulgent, you will find a place that will suit your cravings just right. Here are a few local establishments that you can sample:

Santarpio's Pizza
  Phone:617-567-9871

Santarpio's Pizza is one of the most popular restaurants in Boston. It was first established as a bakery back in 1903. Its original store was located at 111 Chelsea St., East Boston, but they now also have a branch at 71 Newbury St., Peabody.

This pizza place looks a lot like the old town houses from the 1920s—very nostalgic for many folks. Santarpio's serves New York style pizza at an affordable price. You could get a delicious Italian cheese pizza for as low as $10.50. They also serve barbecues, steaks, and sausages, too. This amazing restaurant has an impressive wine list, too. You could eat your pizza with a glass of Burgundy or Chablis.

Craigie on Main
Phone:617-497-5511

Craigie on Main is one of the most popular high end restaurants in Greater Boston. It's located at 853 St., Cambridge. This is a perfect dinner spot if you're doing a day trip to Harvard and MIT.

This restaurant serves some of the best burgers in the city. What makes this burger special is that it's made of beef brisket and bone marrow. The ingredient for which can be quite scarce so the restaurant only serves 18 burgers each night. Make sure to come to the restaurant early!

Bootleg Special
Phone:617-451-1800

Bootleg Special is located at 400 Tremont Street, Boston. It's an industrial space decorated with vibrant chandeliers, vivid carpets, and elegant furniture.

This modern establishment serves some of the most appetizing Cajun-style dishes that would definitely leave you craving for more. They serve tasty dishes that are loaded with shrimps, cheese, crawfish, crabs, lobsters, oysters, clams, and sinful butter. They also have an exquisite wine list.

Cultivar
Phone:617-979-8203

Cultivar offers its guests with the option to dine in a beautiful outdoor seating area. Perfect for balmy Boston summers.

Cultivar was founded by renowned chef Mary Dumont. It's recognized as one of the best restaurants in the city. This restaurant serves a wide array of picture perfect food, including "croquet madame", "malted milk French toast", "rhubarb tart", "fish chowder", "spring vegetable salad", and "flowering herb angel cake".

They also have a bar that can provide guests with an impressive selection of wine. This is a great place for both foodies and wine connoisseurs.

Grill 23
Phone:617-542-2255

If you're a serious steak lover, head out to Grill 23. This is definitely the best steakhouse in Boston. It's a cozy restaurant has been around for more than 30 years. It serves luxury chops that will make you forget your name. It serves familiar comfort food and yet it offers an out of this world gastronomical experience.

Grill 23 is located at 161 Berkeley Street, Boston and meals cost more than $60.

6

The Most Amazing Boston Landmarks

Boston is one of the oldest cities in the United States and as we have established early on, it's also got quite the fascinating history. So, it's no surprise that you can find a number of historical landmarks within it.

The whole city is filled with different architectural gems, interesting land-scapes, and world-renowned universities. In fact, there are more than three hundred landmarks in the city. While you won't be able to see all of them in just a single visit, there are a few that you shouldn't miss out:

Old State House

This historic building stands tall amidst the towering skyscrapers. It's located at the intersection of State and Washington streets. It was built in 1713, making it the oldest public building in Boston. This building was once the seat of the Massachusetts General Court. It also served as Boston's city hall for 11 years and was once a commercial building. It's now a museum and a National Historic Landmark.

Old State House

Trinity Church

The Trinity Church is one the most historic churches in the United States. It is the parish of the Massachusetts Episcopal Diocese.

Trinity Church

This church is known for its exquisite Richardsonian Romanesque architecture. It's grand yet rather quirky at the same time. The building's façade is decorated with arches and statues. Its interior is filled with paintings, elaborate and colorful columns, and stained glass windows. It really is a must-see, especially if you're a fan of architecture.

Boston Common

Boston Common is the oldest city park in the United States. It was established in 1634 and is located in the heart of the city. It has a land area of about 50 acres and is surrounded by Park Street, Beacon Street, Tremont Street, Boylston Street, and Charles Street.

Like many sites in Boston, this park has a rich and interesting history. This stunning park was once the pasture of William Blackstone, the city's first white resident. He's one of the early colonists who arrived in the United States. After some years, and after the original colony returned to England, he moved to an area that the Native Americans called "Shawmut" (which means spring waters). He lived there as a hermit for five years.

When the Puritans arrived in 1930, Blackstone decided to move to Rhode Island and sold his land. His pasture later became a common area for community gatherings. People started calling it "Common". It was also once used for military training and as a cattle feeding area. It was even used for public executions. In more recent times, it has become the site of many anti-slavery and anti-war protests.

There are a few historic sites within the park, including, the Brewer Fountain, the Boston Massacre Memorial, and the Parkman Bandstand. You can also visit the Central Burying Ground where you could see the graves of known local artists, composers, and poets including, Caleb Davis, William Billings, Gilbert Stuart, Charles Sprague, and John Baptiste Julien.

Faneuil Hall Marketplace

Faneuil Hall was completed in 1740, making it one of the oldest landmarks in Boston. It's now part of the marketplace complex, which includes three other buildings – the Quincy Market, North Market, and South Market.

The Faneuil Hall is often called "The Cradle of Liberty" as it is the site patriots, including Sam Adams, delivered speeches encouraging their fellow colonists to stand up against Britain and fight for independence. This hall is so popular that it's ranked as one of the most visited tourist sites in the United States.

Faneuil Hall

This hall was once destroyed by fire in 1761 and it was rebuilt in 1762. It was designed by John Smibert and it was modeled after traditional English country markets. There are a lot of things that you can do in the area. You can see the statue of one of the founding fathers of the United States – Samuel Adams.

You can also eat and shop! You can buy jewelry, shoes, accessories, and specialty gifts. You could find a lot of shops in the area, including Uniqlo, Victoria's Secret, Coach, and Ann Taylor. You could also find a few of street performers during busier days.

Old South Meeting House

This famous landmark is a Congressional church building. But, it's known as the organizing point of one of the most historical events in the United States – the Boston Tea Party.

This building was completed in 1729. After the Boston Massacre, the church became the site of meeting place where famous patriots like Dr. Joseph Warren and John Hancock delivered speeches that urged the colonists to fight for independence.

Old South Meeting House

This building has an old town church vibe. It has a pointed tower that exudes power, elegance, and even mystery.

7

The Five Best Museums in Boston

If the walking tours has left you harkening to learn more about the city and the country's history, then head on over to one of the many esteemed museums within Boston. Allow art, artifacts, and surviving traces of bygone eras teach you more about the past and help you appreciate the present even more.

Boston has over 60 museums that you can visit, but here are some that you shouldn't miss out on:

The Museum of Fine Arts, Boston

Address: 465 Huntington Ave

The Museum of Fine Arts, Boston is one of the buildings that will instantly catch your eye should you start with a walking tour. At the entrance of this building, you'll find the sculpture called the "Appeal to the Great Spirit", which features a Native American man riding on a peaceful-looking stallion. It was created by Cyrus E. Dallin in 1909.

Museum of Fine Arts

The Museum of Fine Arts (Boston) follows a Grecian-style architecture, and is decorated with classic Ionic columns. It was founded in 1870 at a different location and was later moved to its current site in 1909.

The MFA Boston is also one the biggest museums in the United States and it's one of the most popular spots in the city, attracting over a million visitors every year. But, it's so big that it hardly gets crowded. Even on busy days, you still be able to walk freely along its halls.

The museum's truly impressive collection comes from different parts of the world – Africa, Oceania, the Americas, and Europe. You'll find a number of treasures and historical artifacts, including the Dainichi (The Buddha of Infinite Illumination) from 1149, a female effigy jar from 200 BC, tea sets and coffee pots from the 16th century, gold jewelry from 450 AD, and a bust of an Egyptian king from 760 BC.

This museum is open every day; from 10 am to 5 pm on Mondays, Tuesdays, Saturdays, and Sundays. It's open from 10 am to 10 pm on Wednesdays, Thursdays, and Fridays. The admission fee costs $25 as of writing.

Boston Tea Party Ships and Museum

306 Congress St, Boston

The Boston Tea Party is considered by many to be one of American History's turning points. It is the first major act of defiance by the colonists against the British Government, and also played a role in the conception of the American Revolution.

The Boston Tea Party was a non-violent protest and yet, the British responded to this event harshly, which led to the American Revolution. This is the reason why Boston is also known as the "Cradle of Liberty".

Boston Tea Party Ships and Museum

The Boston Tea Party Ships and Museum was built to commemorate this important event. It's an interactive exhibit that both kids and adults can learn plenty from.

This floating museum is located on Congress Street Bridge. It has been voted as the number one museum in Boston, so it's something that you shouldn't miss. You might even chance upon actors reenacting scenes from history! This museum also has a tea room, where you could sit and enjoy a warm cup of tea and your choice of desserts.

This museum has various exhibits, including:

- The Meeting House – This is where you could see a few actors reenact the historical events of 1773 that eventually led to the American Revolution.
- Griffin's Wharf – The wharf has that old street vibe that you'll feel like

you're transported to 1773.

- The Tea Party Ships – On December 1773, the members of the Sons of Liberty went into three docked ships that contained tons of tea from the British East India Company. These ships were called Beaver, Eleanor, and Dartmouth.
- Minuteman Theatre – This is where you can watch a multi-sensory film called "Let it Begin Here". This film depicts the events of April 1775 detailing Paul Revere's ride to alert the arrival of the British forces. This is officially the start of the American Revolution. This is officially the start of the American Revolution.
- The 1773 Tea Chest – The Robinson Tea Chest is known as the only surviving chest during the Boston Tea Party in 1773. This artifact is indeed interesting and it's the symbol of the patriotism of Bostonians.
- Abigail Tea Room and Terrace – This tea room transports you to another era. The waitresses are dressed like it's 1773. You could sample up to five types of teas. You can also order muffins, lemonade, cookies, and different pies.

The museum is open from 10 am to 5 pm and the entrance fee costs about $31.00.

The Mapparium

200 Massachusetts Ave, Boston

Looking for a unique experience? Then the Mapparium might fit the bill. It's basically a three-storey globe that's made of stained glass. It is housed inside the Mary Baker Eddy Library, located at 200 Massachusetts Avenue, Boston. This museum is made of 608 stained-glass panels. It's a 3D representation of what the world looked like in 1935. This museum also uses technology and light to further enhance the experience, making a feast for the senses. Not as popular as other attractions, the Mapparium is definitely one of Boston's less known treasures.

They are open 7 days a week from 10 am to 5 pm, but it's closed during holidays. The admission fee costs $6 as of writing.

Isabela Stewart Gardner Museum
  8WQ2+79 Boston

Isabela Stewart Gardner is considered by many to be one of the most interesting Bostonians. First off, she was an avid art collector. Despite being born in a wealthy family from New York, she was not accepted in the Boston high society. This led her to develop a strong bond with a group of socially alienated artists.

When her son died, she traveled around Europe for three years and was left in awe by the grandeur of the European museums. When she came back to Boston, she hosted many parties and invited artists, musicians, and writers. She also used her inheritance to buy beautiful artworks and began to build her collection. Eventually, she built a museum in 1903.

The Isabela Stewart Gardner Museum is one of the most beautiful and interesting museums not only in Boston, but in the United States. It has a palace-like grandeur, and boasts of a collection that matches rightly with that. They house the works of Giovanni Bellini, Raphael, Pierro Della Francesca, James McNiel Whistler, Gentile Bellini Piero del Pollaiuolo, Edgar Degas, and Francois Boucher. This museum is also filled with priceless artworks from Asia, Medieval Europe, ancient Rome, 19th century France, and around the United States.

True to its founder, the space also hosts contemporary art which features the works of their resident artists. They also have a gallery called The Blue Room which features the artworks of Gardner's closest friends: John Singer Sargent, Ralph Wormeley Curtis, and Joseph Lindon Smith. It also houses Henry James' letter to Isabella Gardner.

The museum was also the site of the infamous "heist of the century"? On March 18, 1990, thirteen valuable artworks were stolen from the museum. These artworks have a combined value of 500 million dollars. The missing artworks, including "The Storm on the Sea of Galilee" by Rembrant and "The Concert" by the famous Dutch painter Johannes Vermeer. This was a truly curious incident, certainly worth looking into when you visit!

Boston Children's Museum
308 Congress St, Boston

Have kids? Then this should be among your first stops! The Boston Children's Museum helps you harness the power of play. It provides a playground that both kids and even adults will enjoy.

This is a place where children can learn about history in a fun way. Kids are also given freedom to construct pipes and buildings. They can even try rock climbing and allow their imaginations to run wild—exactly how it should be.

This museum is located at 308 Congress St., Boston. It's quite easy to find this museum because there's a giant milk statue in front of it. It is open from 10 am to 5 am on Saturday to Thursday. It's open until 10 pm on Fridays. Entrance fee costs $17.

8

The Best Art Galleries in Boston

We've tackled museums that give people a glimpse into history, now let's look into what the art scene in the city is like. Boston has its fair share of great art galleries. If you're a little limited when it comes to time, here's the top 5 you have to see before leaving town:

Galerie d'Orsay

Galerie d' Orsay is located at 33 Newsbury St., Boston. It's at the heart of the famous Boston Back Bay. This gallery was established in 2000 and houses modern art from some of the biggest names throughout the decades.

Their collection includes pieces of artworks by well-known artists, such as Pablo Picasso, Andy Warhol, Harmensz Van Rijn Rembrandt, Anne McGory, Jules Cheret, Pierre Auguste Renoir, and Camille Pissarro. This gallery also held various art exhibitions which featured the works of Kathy Buist, Natasha Zupan, Bruno Zupan, Joan Miro, Mary Cassatt, and Alexander Calder.

The Iris Gallery of Fine Art of Photography

Located at 129 Newbury St, Boston is the Iris Gallery of Fine Art. It's quite near Galerie d'Orsay so you can visit both within the same day. The Iris was founded in 2004 by Alison Collins and features the amazing photographs of Jean Michel Berts, Fred Collins, Peter Daitch, Lisa Cueman, Ormond Gigli, Peter Garfield, Andrezj Pluta, and Joanne Schmaltz.

It is also the home to several art installations, including: Bowthorpe by Beth Moon, Sailing Images by Michael Khan, Head of Harbor by Peter Daitch, 8 Ball by Fred Collins, and the Avenue of Oaks by Beth Moon.

Krakow Witkin Gallery
10 Newbury St, Boston

Considered by many to be among the most prestigious galleries in Boston, the Krakow Witkin Gallery was founded in in 1964. It features post-modernist work, including the wor of various artists, such as Mel Bochner, Josef Albers, Julian Opie, Alex Katz, Ed Ruscha, Lorna Simpson, Sarah Sze, John Wesley, Paolo Ventura, Michael Mazur, Mike Glier, and Sally B. Moore.

The gallery may look cold at first glance, but spend time in it and you'll find that the art brings warmth to the space.

Hidden Art Gallery

The Hidden Art Gallery is located at 25 Myrtle St, right at the heart of Beacon Hill. Their current collection features the work Zoe Arguello, Patrick Anderson, Anne Foresman, and Hannah Groudas. They also regularly host various charitable events, which happens every first Friday of the month.

Gallery Kayafas

Gallery Kayafas is located at 450 Harrison Avenue. This gallery is simple and yet, it showcases thought-provoking and rare artworks. It opened in 2002 and owned by Arlette Kayafas. It features the works of Jules Aarons, Teenie Harris, Geoff Hargadon, Julie Miller, Tim Donovan, Frank Gohlke, and Lynn Saville.

9

Boston: A Coffee Lover's Paradise

Sure, there's a lot of Starbucks in Boston. You could find one on Beacon St, another one on Atlantic Avenue, and one in 63 -65 Court Street. But, if you want to have a unique local coffee experience in Boston, head out to the best Boston coffee shops listed below.

Tamper

Tamper is located at 340 Boston Avenue. It opens at 7:30 am and closes at 3:00 pm. But, the café serves dinner every Wednesday from 6 to 9 pm.

Tamper Café serves affordable espressos, cappuccinos, lattes, and even teas. They also serve cold brew coffee, home-made soda, and beers. If you want a light meal or a simple snack, they have egg sandwiches, chicken pesto, quiche, grilled cheese, and tuna melt sandwich. Tamper's got an impressive dinner menu, too.

Thinking Cup

Thinking Cup is located downtown, just a few steps away from the city park

Boston Common. It is the usual hangout of busy Boston locals, particularly the students, hence the name.

The Thinking Cup sources coffee beans from all over the world, so their coffee has rich and interesting flavors. They have a team of great coffee artists, too. This café has a modern interior. It's cozy. But, what makes this café special is the level of its service. Definitely ten times better than Starbucks. The baristas take their time to inform their customers about the different coffee beans and their flavors.

Cuppacoffee

This is an Australian coffee shop that serves delicious macchiatos, lattes, espresso, and house blends. This coffee shop has an extremely cozy industrial interior. This coffee shop is located at 1 Merrimac St, Boston.

Cuppacoffee has three locations in Boston. There's one in 57 Traveler St., another one in 1 Merrimar St., and one in 699 Boylston St.

Crema Café

This hip coffee shop is located at 27 Brattle St., Cambridge and it attracts the Harvard crowd. This café has a homey atmosphere, perfect for study sessions or simply hanging out with friends. The café serves different types of coffee, such as café au lait, espresso, golden crema, chai latte, red crema, mate latte, macchiato, and cappuccino.

They also have quiche, fresh fruit salad, bagel with cream cheese, red quinoa bowl, and pesto muffin on the menu.

Gracenote Coffee

Gracenote Coffee is located at Lincoln Street between the South Station, the Financial District, and Chinatown. It has a convenient location, so it's popular among Boston commuters.

They greet guests with a simple and yet, cozy interior. A great spot for winding down after a long day. This popular coffee shop serves fresh and delicious coffee and they do coffee art, too.

10

The Best Bars and Pubs in Boston

Boston is home to many stylish and homey bars. If you're looking for a drink that's a bit stronger than your usual cup of coffee, head on over to the popular spots listed below:

JM Curley

This is a popular hangout for yuppies and students. It's located at 21 Temple Pl. It gives off a relaxed yet cool vibe, so a lot of Bostonians visit this place after a long workday.

They also offer interesting cocktail mixes, including: yellow charteuse, soda, lunazel tequila, cinnamon, espresso, bourbon, maraschino, Aztec chocolate, rosemary, citadille gin, ginger, and apple juice.

JM Curley is also a favorite among the picky beer drinkers. They have an extensive list of unique beers and brews, including Prima Pils, Bengali, Original Cider, Orval, Weisse, Rocherfort 6, Tecate, Gansett, and Brooklyn Lager.

They also serve steaks, poached eggs, French toast, fries, Jalapenos, and veggie burger. So, it's a hug for vegetarian, too.

Wink & Nod

located on Appleton St., Boston this lounge is actually frequented by tourists and many office workers after they clock out. The lounge offers a number of cocktails, such as the "cumin knock on my door", "into the wild", "open sesame", "la fantasma", "la paloma", and "Persian summer". These cocktails contain ingredients like apple brandy, pomegranate, tequila, ginger beer, honey, yogurt, curacao, orange oil, bourbon, and whisky.

Want something truly indulgent? Try their 100 dollar cocktail called the "billionaire bijou". This cocktail contains expensive ingredients such as Chartreuse VEP, Orange Bitters, Saffron Boutique, Gilded Cherry, and Rose Water.

Lookout Rooftop and Bar

This marvelous bar sits at the very top of the Envoy Hotel and provides guests with a stunning view of the bay. It's located at 70 Sleeper St. in the stunning seaport district. The bar serves delicious and Instagram-worthy cocktails—perfect for people who enjoy documenting everything! They also have excellent pancakes, burgers, and fries.

This bar is open from 4 pm to 12 am every Mondays, Tuesdays, and Wednesdays. It's open until midnight from Thursday to Saturday. It's open from 12 noon to 11 pm every Sundays.

Brendan Behan Pub

This Irish pub is located at 378 Centre St. in the historic neighborhood of Jamaica Plain. It's the haven for serious beer drinkers—not surprising given their selection of draft beers, including "Guiness", "Jack's Abby", "Lost Nation", "Beerworks Pumpkin", "Stone Go To", "Brooklyn", and "Clown Shoes Clementine". They also serve fun drinks like "Sweaty Betty", "Fernet Branca", "Apple Ginger", "Crypt Keeper", "Mezcal", and "Fireball".

This pub exudes nothing but good vibes. It is no doubt the best Irish bar in Boston.

Delux Café

This bar has that hippie All-American vibe, complete with comfortable leather furniture and images of Elvis—the iconic king of rock and roll. Located at 100 Chandler St., Boston, it's certainly one of the most popular dive bars in town. They serving a selection of drinks, from alcoholic to non-alcoholic.

If you're looking for an easy time with friends or want something more at home, and relaxed—this is the spot to go to.

11

Boston Nightlife: Top Spots For Locals

Boston nightlife is mostly wild and electrifying; consider the fact that they have the largest number of millenials in any given US city, that alone should explain why. Whether you're a hardcore party animal, a social drinker, or a Latin dance lover, there's a nightclub in Boston that fits your partying style.

The Grand Boston

The Grand Boston is one of the hippest clubs in Boston. This high energy club is located at 58 Seaport Boulevard Suite 300 and it's called Grand Boston for a reason. This place screams luxury. It's a hedonist's paradise. It provides a feast for the senses – good music, great ambience, and an exciting crowd. You'll even find DJ Steve Aoki playing music at this club on some nights. How awesome is that? This place is amazing, wild, and elegant all at the same time. If indulgence is what you're after, give this place a shot.

Royale

Royale looks like a posh theatre. It's located at 279 Tremont St., Boston and even at first glance, everything about this place exudes mystery and elegance. It has comfortable couches where you could sit and just sip your cocktail.

On some days, this club is also transformed into a concert venue where popular bands and DJs perform. The lights are captivating and the cocktail menu is impressive. The club even employs aerial dancers and acrobats to provide the guests a one of a kind party experience. Royale is a place where yuppies and local college kids party and let out some steam.

Emerald Lounge

Located in the Best Western Oasis Inn at 200 Stuart St., Boston, the most notable detail of this lounge is in the name itself. The place is bathed in green light—refreshing and energizing.

The Emerald Lounge has an interesting industrial design and they showcase an eye-catching installation artwork as their centerpiece. It also has a cozy patio where you could just hang out if you don't feel like dancing. The crowd is not as wild compared to the Grand Boston or Royale, but it's a good place to dance, meet new people, and just have an amazing time.

Havana Club

If you love Salsa dancing, head to the Havana Club. This is if you're looking for something other than your usual night club. This place doesn't play overrated electronic music. Instead, you'll be treated to some classic Cuban flavors and learn salsa while you're at it. This place exudes contagious positive vibes and a different energy compared to the other places. It's definitely a must-try for couples, too!

Whisky Saigon

Whisky Saigon is representative of the diverse and vibrant Boston nightlife. The club exudes a luxurious Eastern vibe. Whisky Saigon also has an amazing dance area, often filled with hypnotizing music and bright lights. It's also the site of many fashion shows, product launches, and vodka parties. It's a haven for the locals who are looking for something sophisticated but without losing the spirit of spontaneity and fun.

This blazing club is located at 116 Boylston, Boston.

12

Things That You Can Only Do In Boston

Every city will always have something that is uniquely their own. The same rings true for Boston. There are many touristy things you can do, but there are a few that you can only enjoy within the city. For first-timer visitors, consider this your initiation—an introduction to what the town has to offer.

Walk the Freedom Trail

The freedom trail is a path made of red bricks. This trail is 2.5 miles long and it is the home of sixteen of the most historic landmarks in Boston. The trail starts at the Boston Common and ends at the Bunker Hill Monument in Charlestown.

Here's the list of historical spots and landmarks that you can see in this area:

- **The Boston Common** - This is the oldest public park in the United States, which was established in 1634.

- **The Massachusetts State** – This architectural wonder is certainly easy on the eyes. It conveys intellect and power. Its most distinguishing feature is the gold dome. Yes, the entire dome is covered with actual 24 karat gold. This state house was built in 1798, making it the oldest continually functioning state capital building in the United States.

Massachusetts State House

- **Robert Gould Shaw Memorial** – This is a statue depicts Robert Gould Shaw, who led a battalion of African American soldiers known as the 54th Regiment.

- **The Patrick St. Church** – This church was established in 1809 and it was also the first Sunday school in the United States.

- **The Granary Ground** – This is the final resting place of famous patriots, including Paul Revere, Samuel Adams, James Otis, Robert Treat Paine, and John Hancock. This cemetery looks eerie, but it also looks serene and incredibly glorious.

Granary Ground

- **The King's Chapel** – This small church was built in 1688. It has a simple stone façade. But, if make sure to go inside and see the bell made by the great Paul Revere. As you know, this patriot is also a silversmith.

- **Boston Latin School** – This school was established in 1635, making it the oldest school in the United States.

- **The Old City Hall** – This building used to be the seat of the city council. It has a granite exterior. It is considered as a historical and architectural treasure. It also used to be the office of John F. Fitzgerald, John F. Kennedy's grandfather.

Old City Hall

- **Old South Meeting House** – This church used to be the meeting place of the Sons of Liberty.

- **Old Corner Bookstore** – This is a simple building, but it has a great story. It was established in 1712. It used to be the meeting place of brilliant minds like Harriet Beecher Stowe and Ralph Waldo Emerson.

- **Old State House** – This building was established in 1713 and it used to be the center of Colonial Boston. It's open from 9 am to 5 pm and the admission fee costs $10.

Old State House

- **Boston Massacre Memorial** – This memorial depicts the five American colonists who died during the Boston Massacre in March 5, 1770.

- **Feneuil Hall** – This is considered as the "cradle of liberty". This historical landmark was modeled after the London Royal Exchange Building.

- **<u>Paul Revere House</u>** – Paul Revere is the famous Bostonian who in April 18, 1775 rode on a horse and warned his compatriots of the arrival of the British forces. After the war, Paul Revere returned to his career as a silversmith and became a famous industrialist.

Paul Revere House

- **Paul Revere Statue** – This statue depicts Paul Revere riding a horse and warning his fellow men of the arrival of the British forces. This monument is located near the statue.

- **The U.S.S. Constitution Museum** – This ship (turned museum) is the oldest commissioned ship in the United States. It's definitely one of the most interesting and beautiful museums in the United States. The U.S.S. Constitution is historical, too. It's more than 200 years old and it marks the start of the US Navy.

· **Bunker Hill Monument**

The last stop would the Bunker Hill Monument, which is the site of one of the first major battles between the American Patriots and the British Forces.

Bunker Hill Monument

You can do the Freedom Trail tour by yourself or opt to join one of the many tour groups.

Explore One of the Greatest Universities in the World: Harvard

If you're in Boston City for three to five days, you should take a day trip to Cambridge and see one of the greatest (if not the greatest) university in the world – Harvard.

Harvard

Harvard is the alma mater of many great men and women, including Theodore Roosevelt, Franklin Delano Roosevelt, John F. Kennedy, George W. Bush, Al Gore, Larry Summers, Barack Obama, E.E. Cummings, Ralph Waldo Emerson, and Helen Keller. It was also home to some of the most successful college dropouts like Bill Gates, Mark Zuckerberg (but, he has an honorary degree),

Robert Frost, Dustin Moskovitz, and Matt Damon.

Harvard is a place where dreams come true for many students. It is the training ground for many great businessmen, some of the most prolific politicians, and the most talented writers and academics. That said, it is also a popular tourist spot. There are a lot of things to see in Harvard, including:

· **Harvard Square**

This plaza is adjacent to the Harvard Yard. It's located at the intersection of John F. Kennedy St., Brattle St., and Massachusetts Avenue. This square is certainly quite picturesque, especially if you visit during the autumn months. There, you would be able to find streets lined with quaint coffee shops, bookstores, and shops.

· The Widener Library

The Widener Library is definitely one of the best libraries in the world. It boasts of an impressive Greek revival architectural design which is quite a sight to behold if you love design. Its impressive collection of books matches the grand exterior aptly. You can easily lose a couple of hours just wandering around in there and feeding the bookworm in you.

· Harvard Yard

This grassy open space is one of the oldest parts of Harvard, but don't let that fool you into thinking it's a bore. This spot is great for picnics and ball games. The yard is also surrounded by libraries and freshman dormitories.

It also houses the Memorial Church, a number of classrooms, and the offices of the university dean and president. Here you'll find the statue of John Harvard, the British minister who founded Harvard University. But, here's one curious fact about the statue— no one really knows what John Harvard looked like and so, Sherman Hoaf became the inspiration for the statue's face.

Harvard School Of Business

· <u>The Harvard Museum of Natural History (HMNH)</u>

This museum can be easily recognized by its imposing red façade. It was established in 1998 and is home to hundreds of sea creatures, glass flowers, and fossils. It also has an extensive collection of mounted animals, which includes a jaguar, a giant armadillo, and a sloth.

· <u>Peabody Museum of Archaeology and Ethnology</u>

This museum is located just across HMNH. It was founded in 1866, making it one of the oldest anthropological museums.

The Peabody Museum of Archaeology and Ethnology has an extensive collection of artifacts, including Native American art, bronze plaques from Africa, and gold plaques from Panama.

Harvard is not only a university, it's also a living piece of history. A simple walk through the campus is an experience in itself, especially when you think about all the great minds that have passed through the same path you're now treading. Spare a whole day for this trip, it will be well worth it!

Take A Tour Around MIT

The Massachusetts Institute of Technology should also be part of your Cambridge day trip. You may know the university as the home to some of the most brilliant and innovative minds in the world. It has a long and impressive list of successful graduates, including company presidents, CEO, prime ministers, physicists, company founders, scientists, and entrepreneurs.

MIT

This prestigious university is the home to many creative minds, so it's no surprise that the campus is a bit quirky. It's currently home to many architectural curiosities, such as the oval-shaped Kresge Auditorium, the solemn MIT chapel, and the famous Ray and Maria Stata Center.

During your visit, make sure you stop by the MIT Museum. This thought-provoking museum has an extensive collection of holograms, memorabilias, and MIT hacks archives. It also showcases many old photographs that depict the history, various events, and student life at MIT.

Visit Fenway Park

Fenway Park is the home of the Boston Red Sox. It's a haven for baseball fans worldwide. There's plenty to learn here about the sport and the many great names that are associated with it so it's certainly worth a visit!

Fenway Park

Fenway Park was built in 1911 by former Red Sox owner John I. Taylor. The first game in the park was played on April 20, 1912, which was between the Boston Red Sox and the New York Highlanders. Since then, this stadium has become one of the popular landmarks in the city.

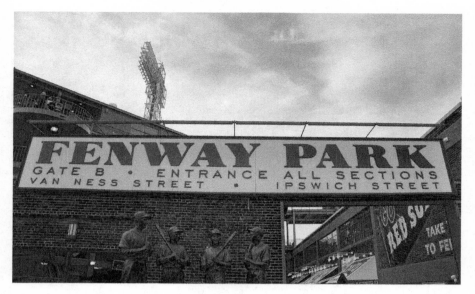

Ride a Swan Boat at the Public Garden

4 Charles St S, Boston

Phone: +1 617-522-1966

Riding a swan tour boat is one of the most "touristy" things that you can do in Boston. The swan boats were built in 1877 and are considered to be a cultural icon for the city. It certainly is the most recognizable and even locals will tell you that it's a must-do.

Swan Boat

A swan boat tour gives you different look of the public garden, one that's more relaxing and quite romantic too. After all, you will find real swans joining you while you cruise along. This is an activity that both children and adults will enjoy!

13

Safety and Insider Travel Tips

When it comes to any type of trip, safety is always a priority. Boston, much like other cities in the country, does have its fair share of crime. This is something you can avoid by being a smarter traveler, of course, and doing ample research before you go. That said, here's what you need to know:

Most crimes in Boston are drug-related, so avoid walking alone in parks at night. Stick to the busier, more populated areas instead. Also, it's best to avoid the "bad neighborhoods" like Dorchester, Roxbury, and Mattapan. Yes, it isn't always the best to label certain areas as unsafe but these locales do have their reputations. Better safe than sorry, right?

Don't carry a lot of cash when you're walking around and make sure you're always aware of your valuables, especially if you're in a bus or a train. There are a number of pickpockets in public transportation and in tourist spots as well.

Aside from that here's a list of other travel tips that you can use to stay safe and make the most out of your Boston vacation:

- Don't compare the Red Sox to the Yankees. It's just rude.

- It's difficult to get a decent parking area around the city. So, don't rent a car. The best way to explore the city is by foot or public transportation.

- Avoid the tourist traps – the fake historic places. You could find a lot of fake historical places at the Quincy market.

- The city has a bike lane. So, make don't bike on the sidewalk, it's illegal.

· If you want your coffee black, you have to tell the barista that you like black coffee. The "regular coffee" in Boston usually has a lot of cream.

Boston is generally a safe city. But, like most mega cities, it has a share of pickpockets and thieves, too. Also, do avoid the tourist traps – and always look around for the best bargains if you're out shopping for local specialties and offerings. And most of all, have fun and enjoy everything this vibrant city has to offer.

Emergency Phone: 911

14

The Ultimate Boston 3 Day Travel Itinerary

Given every recommendation we've provided above, it's plain to see that there's lots of things you can enjoy in Boston. But, if you're only in the city for three days, here's a fool-proof itinerary that you can use to make the most out of your short stay.

Day 1 – Gardens and Freedom Trail Tour

You should not leave Boston without seeing the most historical buildings and landmarks.

From the airport, take the bus to the city's center via the SL1 bus. To make the most of your time, it's best to pick a hotel near Beacon Hill.

Here's a list of sites that you should visit:

Boston Public Garden – This garden looks divine during the summer and autumn. You could go around the garden or you could ride the swan boat to get a good view of the garden's beauty and splendor. You can spend 45 minutes to

1 hour in this garden.

Boston Public Garden

The Freedom Trail – Spend most of your afternoon walking the Freedom trail. See the famous landmarks in the area, including the Granary Burial Ground, Bunker Hill Monument, Old South Meeting House, the Boston Massacre Monument, the USS Constitution Museum, the Faneuil Hall Marketplace, the Paul Revere House, and the Old North Church.

Faneuil Hall

If you have more time, visit the stunning Trinity Church in Back Bay. Then, head to the nearby shopping centers. As mentioned earlier in this book, Back Bay is the top shopping district in Boston.

After a long day, you can head to the hippest bars or night clubs in the city to unwind and just have a good time.

Day 2 – Day Trip to Cambridge – Harvard and MIT

You can take the train or bus to Cambridge from Boston. You can also rent a car and drive all the way there.

You can explore Harvard by yourself or you can opt to join the guided historical tours. These tours usually last for an hour and they're free! They're great if you're keen on learning more as you explore the surroundings.

MIT

After exploring Harvard, you can eat lunch at one of the hippest restaurants in the area and then, head to the other educational gem of Cambridge – MIT. It's just four minutes away from Harvard.

You could also do a guided tour around MIT. The afternoon tour begins at 2:30 pm, but you have to make a reservation by calling 617 -253 – 7669.

Day 3 – Museum and Sports

Before you leave Boston, be sure that you leave some time to explore its museums, art galleries, and cafes. Visit the Isabella Steward Gardner Museum to view their impressive collection and learn more about the greatest art heist in the United States. Then, head to the Museum of Fine Arts. This is great for winding down after your adventures around the city.

Boston Tea Party Ships and Museum

Have lunch and then, head to the Boston Tea Party Ships and Museum. This is something you shouldn't miss as there's plenty to learn and see. If you're traveling with kids, it's a good idea to also visit the Children's Museum and the New England Aquarium.

Lastly, relive some of baseball's greatest moments at Fenway Park; this is a must for both sports enthusiasts and casual fans of the sport.

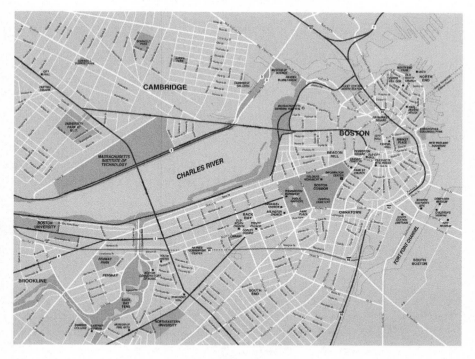

15

Conclusion

Thank you for downloading this book!

Boston is one of the most amazing cities in the world. It is compact, clean, and it has a rich and interesting history. It's a city that you should visit at least once in your lifetime.

Here are a few tips that you can use when visiting Boston:

- Wear comfortable clothes, you're going to walk a lot.
- Don't buy a Charlie ticket. Buy a Charlie card instead. You'll save 55 cents per ride.
- Don't bring a car or rent one. It's hard to drive around the city as there are a lot of one-way streets. It's also quite easy to get lost. The best way to get around Boston is by foot or public transportation.
- Skip the tourist traps. There are a lot of fake historical spots in Boston. If it's not in the guidebooks and history books, it's probably fake.
- There are a lot of free walking tours around the city, take advantage of that.
- Check the tour schedules in Harvard and MIT before traveling to Cambridge.
- If you like your coffee black, you have to say it. Don't say that you like "regular coffee". The regular coffee in Boston usually has a lot of cream and it comes with a coffee art, too.
- Boston has a lot of restaurants, but only a few fast food joints. So, ditch the fast food and eat real food.
- The clam chowder in Boston is the best in the world. You should try it.
- Hold on to your bag and important belongings if you're in a bus or a train.
- Do not walk in parks alone after dark.
- If you want to avoid huge crowds, head to the Sound End part of Boston.

And lastly, have fun! Boston is a good place to learn new things, enjoy everything that the Athens of America has to offer.

Thank you again for downloading this book and good luck!

16

Thank You

I want to thank you for reading this book! I sincerely hope that you received value from it!

If you received value from this book, I want to ask you for a favour. Would you be kind enough to leave a review for this book on Amazon?

CLICK HERE TO GO TO AMAZON

indirectly.

Respective authors own all copyrights not held by the publisher.

The information herein is offered for informational purposes solely, and is universal as so. The presentation of the information is without contract or any type of guarantee assurance.

The trademarks that are used are without any consent, and the publication of the trademark is without permission or backing by the trademark owner. All trademarks and brands within this book are for clarifying purposes only and are the owned by the owners themselves, not affiliated with this document.

Made in the USA
Las Vegas, NV
24 July 2022

52028758R00062